STEPS ON BREAD MAKING

A book for knowledge and aquitaintancy

Keep every book safe from harsh weather for a prolonged lifespan.

INTRODUCTION

Whether you're new to making bread or just need a little refresher course, these bread making primer will answer all your questions about making bread. Paired with additional resources and recipes, this primer will have you feeling like a culinary genius in no time.

TABLE OF CONTENTS

I. Essential Tools For Making Bread…………I

II. Ingredients For Making Bread……………..II

III. Steps On How to Make Bread……………..III

IV. Running Through The Process…………….IV

Bread have become one of the most demanding commodity today in the society because of it's response to our immediate satisfaction. Many people these days prefer to consume this commodity majorly in the morning rather than cooking in order to safe time.

Will be learning how to make this wild spreading food and what is needed to produce it. They are category of equipment used in making bread, we have equipment for manual production of bread with is a bathing tube. Some of the other equipment are;

1. MIXER- this is a bowl-like object that has a roller inside, it has the capacity to mix two bags of flour together at a time. This equipment is used for kneading bread dough.

2. SCALE AND KNIFE- this is used for measuring and cutting of the dough to determine the same weight. With the scale you can determine the price of your profit and loss.
3. OVEN- this is used for baking the already risen bread dough.
4. PAN- this is responsible for the shape of the bread after bake. It is used for housing and shaping the bread.

INGREDIENTS

When it comes to making bread, you will find that there are certain essentials you can never bake without. From choosing the right flour to using proofing bags and dough conditioner, these are lots of nifty kitchen gadgets that will make your life much easier and specific ingredients that will make your bread the masterpiece it deserves to be.

These essentials that will give your bread a good taste and a smart look after production include;

1. Flour
2. Sugar
3. Salt
4. Yeast

5. Butter

With these super ingredients, there is a chance of making a great taste of bread with lots of nutrients everyday. This is not all I have got for you, I shall be taking you to another level where you will learn how to put all these ingredients in place to make the loaves. Water and milk are also necessary.

STEPS ON HOW TO MAKE BREAD

I. **MIX THE BREAD DOUGH**-whether you are making bread in a bread machine, a Stand-type mixer or by hand, the most important ingredient to remember when mixing the dough is the yeast. It's sensitive to temperature and it's relation to other ingredients. Just make sure not to over-mix the dough if you're using a Stand-type mixer.

If you're making your bread in a bread machine, the water should be 80 degrees. If you're making bread in the oven, water should be 110 degrees. Getting the right temperature for your water ensures that you'll have the right temperature in the dough for the yeast to actively grow.

When mixing the ingredients, remember that sugar accelerates the yeast growth while salt kills the yeast. Be sure to keep the salt and the yeast on opposite sides of mixing bowl and get exact measurements of each of your ingredients, the salt especially.

II. KNEAD THE BREAD DOUGH-the important part of kneading is, giving the dough the elasticity it needs to rise. This can be achieved by using a dough hook in the Stand-type mixer or by hand. Your bread machine will automatically go through this process for you. It takes about 15 minutes to knead the dough by hand and 5-10 minutes with a Stand-type mixer.

To knead the dough by hand, simply press the heals of your hand into the dough and pull the dough back over itself only to press the heals of your hand back into the dough again. Repeat until the bread dough becomes elastic.

The way you know when you're done kneading is when you can pinch a portion of the dough and stretch it into smooth, thin layer before it breaks.

With the Stand-type mixer, the sticky dough will completely pull away from the sides of the bowl into a drier ball. When kneading, you may need to adjust for stickiness or dryness according to your bread recipe. You will need to pay close attention throughout the process or your bread could turnout less than perfect.

III. **LETTING THE DOUGH RISE**-the important thing about letting your dough rise is that, it needs to double in size or else it will turn out flat and dense. There's no precise expectation of time for this because it depends on the temperature of your kitchen.

The ideal temperature of a quicker rise is 79 degrees and it could rise in as little as 45 minutes. To control the temperature and environment better and trap in the moisture and heat, we like to advise you to use proofing bags to cover your dough as it rises.

When you let your bread rise for an extended period of time, retarding the rise with cooler temperature, more flavor is developed in the bread making it taste just like a loaf of artesian bread.

IV. **FORM THE BREAD LOAF-** the easiest way to form a bread loaf is by pretending the dough has a ball around it's center to create a smooth surface and tuck the seams into the bottom. Pinch the seams together firmly and put the loaf seam-side down into the pan.

Once your loaf has been formed, set it aside to rise for the second time, this time watch for it to double in size and for air bubbles to rise to rush the loaf into oven.

V. **BAKE THE BREAD-**the important part of baking bread is the internal temperature. It's the only true way that you can know when your bread is done baking. Most bread mixes and recipes will call for a 350 degrees oven.

VI. At this temperature, most loaves will take in about 25 minutes and rolls will bake in 15-20 minutes. Use a kitchen thermometer to check the internal temperature to know when your bread loaf is completely done. You can stick it into the center through the bottom of your loaf.

Your bread is done baking, when the internal temperature reaches 195 degrees for regular loaves or 210 for crusty artisan loaves. If your bread isn't done yet, simply stick it back into the oven and cover it with tin foil to finish baking.

Use these method to carry out this simple techniques for making bread. Please endeavor to pay close attention throughout the process so as not to ruin everything you are producing.

Use Only the Best Bread Flour for Making Bread

Flour is specialized. Bread flour is for making bread and pastry flour is for making cookies and cakes. Professional bakeries rarely use all-purpose flour which is a compromise. Do not use all-purpose flour for bread; it doesn't have enough protein to form the gluten.

We recommend bread flour with 11% or more protein. After trying many bread flours, we use Harvest King by General Mills nearly exclusively in our white breads. Use it if you can find it. For "whole wheat" we use General Mills Stone Ground Whole Wheat Flour.

If over 40% whole wheat, we add more wheat protein (marketed as "gluten") to the flour. We never exceed 40% rye flour in our rye breads and usually add wheat protein to the flour.

Gluten is formed from the protein in the flour. The more protein, all else being equal, the more gluten your bread dough will have and the more capacity it will have to capture gas expelled by the yeast. Gluten causes the elasticity of the bread dough and creates the chewy texture we love in bread.

Kneading the Bread Dough: How Gluten is Formed Now for a little nerdy science. Wheat flour contains two important proteins: gliadin and glutenin. When these proteins are hydrated and worked mechanically–kneaded–

the two proteins combine with water to form tiny strands of gluten that link and crosslink to form a microscopic mesh that captures gas causing the dough to expand.

Making bread is all about maximizing gluten formation. A good dough conditioner will assist by improving extensibility and the ability to capture gas.

A good dough conditioner will also make the bread more acidic, which yeast prefers, and is slightly hygroscopic, slowing the staling of the bread

Dough conditioners are proprietary products and not all are equal. We add dough conditioner to all our bread mixes and have found that dough with conditioner adds another inch in loaf height and therefore lighter, airier bread.

How to Knead the Dough

As explained, kneading the bread is important to maximize the gluten in the dough. It's an essential step in making bread. You can knead the bread with the dough hook in your stand-type mixer, in a bread machine, or by hand.

I grew up kneading bread by hand. It takes about 15 minutes to knead bread by hand. It's easier to show than to tell, but to knead your dough by hand, you press the heels of your hands into the dough and pull the dough back over itself to press the heals of your hands back into the dough again.

Depending on the speed of the machine, it takes six or eight minutes to knead the bread with your mixer and dough hook. The gluten is formed sufficiently when it becomes stretchy and elastic.

Grab the dough between your thumb and forefinger and pull. It should be stretchy enough that you pull the dough into a thin band before it breaks. I love kneading the dough by hand—when I have the time.

There's something about doing it by hand that is personal and brings you closer to the bread-making process with more appreciation for your bread. Of course, your bread machine will do the kneading for you.

Let the Bread Dough Rise Until Nearly Doubled

Bread is organic; cookies and muffins are chemical. Yeast spores are alive and like most other living organisms; they multiply, feed, and expel waste.

In the right environment—warm and moist—the number of organisms will double about every ten minutes. At the end of the rise, there is a lot more yeast in your dough than at the start. The ideal temperature for yeast growth is 79 degrees.

Yeast has the ability to convert the starches in the dough to sugars for energy. That's why breads without sugar, such as French bread, work. The yeast expels a liquid which converts to a gas, carbon dioxide, and alcohol. The alcohol gives bread it's yeasty flavor and the gas makes the dough expand and rise.

So this first rise gives the yeast a chance to become active and multiply and allows the gas and the alcohol to disperse through the dough. Generally, you want to let that process work until the volume of the dough as nearly doubled.

How long that takes is a function of how warm your kitchen is. It is important to cover your dough while it rises so that the surface does not dry and become inelastic.

It is common to stretch plastic over the top of the bowl. But if the bread rises up to the plastic, it will impede the rise of the bread dough. A better answer is to use a proofing bag. A proofing bag is a large plastic bag in which you place your bread bowls or pans, close, and let your dough rise—a mini greenhouse. We sell proofing bags.

They are 32 inches long, so you can slide a baking sheet of rolls into one. Forming the Loaves, the Second Rise, and Knowing When to Put the Bread in the Oven Forming the Loaves Whether you're making a free-standing loaf, dinner rolls, or a loaf in a pan; it's all the same for forming a basic loaf.

Pull the dough around its center— as if it has a ball in the middle, tuck the seams into the bottom of the loaf, and place the dough into the pan.

The Second Rise

This is the rise that counts. This determines how good your bread is going to be. Don't worry about the time. Let it rise until the dough is full of gas. It will be puff and soft.

If you gently poke it with your finger, a little dent will remain. Watch for air bubbles rising to the surface. They will continue to expand until they become blisters.

As soon as you see bubbles under the surface of the dough, it's time to bake. If blisters have formed, poke them with a toothpick and hurry your loaves to the oven. Make sure to hold it with care in order not to have them destroyed, the outlook of it will be pleasant to see after baking.

CONCLUSION

This is where we draw the cotton close, but we are not done yet. We will be bringing to your reach exciting books on varieties of recipes, Thank you for your interest in our books.

www.ingramcontent.com/pod-product-compliance
Lightning Source LLC
Chambersburg PA
CBHW031525210526
45464CB00007B/3026